the WOk book

charmaine solomon

HAMLYN

A Metric/Imperial guide to Australian solid and liquid measures

Liquid measures

Australian	Metric	Imperial
1 cup	250 ml	8 fl oz
½ cup	125 ml	4 fl oz
⅓ cup	75 ml	3 fl oz

Solid measures

Australian	Metric	Imperial
1 cup	300 g	10 oz
½ cup	150 g	5 oz
⅓ cup	125 g	4 oz

Liquid measures/teaspoons/tablespoons
A teaspoon holds approximately 5 ml in both Australia and Britain. The British standard tablespoon holds 15 ml whilst the Australian holds 20 ml.

Australian	British
1 teaspoon	1 teaspoon
1 tablespoon	1 tablespoon
2 tablespoons	2 tablespoons
3½ tablespoons	3 tablespoons
4 tablespoons	3½ tablespoons

Note
Convert cup measures to metric or imperial measure where necessary. Use one set of measurements only and not a mixture. Standard level teaspoon measurements are used in all recipes. Eggs should be medium (size 3) unless otherwise stated.
Milk should be full fat unless otherwise stated.
Pepper should be freshly milled unless otherwise stated.
Fresh herbs should be used unless otherwise stated. If unavailable use dried herbs as an alternative but halve the quantities stated.
For ease of reference:
capsicum = pepper
eggplant = aubergine
zucchini = courgette

First published in Great Britain in 1995
by Hamlyn an imprint of
Reed International Books Limited
Michelin House, 81 Fulham Road
London SW3 9RB

Reprinted 1998

First published in 1993 by Hamlyn Australia
as part of Charmaine Solomon's Asian
Cooking Library

Produced and published in Australia by
New Holland Publishers (Australia) Pty Ltd
Sydney • London • Cape Town

3/2 Aquatic Drive Frenchs Forest NSW 2086
Australia

24 Nutford Place London WIH 6DQ
United Kingdom

80 McKenzie Street Cape Town 8001
South Africa

ISBN 0 600 59027 5

A CIP catalogue for this book is available from the
British Library

Designed by Guy Mirabella
Photographs by Michael Cook
Styling by Margaret Alcock
Food cooked by Nina Harris, Jill Pavey
China by Villeroy & Boch, Australia, Pty Ltd
Printed and bound by Creative Printing Limited,
Hong Kong

contents

introduction

The wok is, I would say, the most popular cooking utensil in the world … not only is it the mainstay of Chinese kitchens but, by one name or another, you will find it throughout Asia.

Western manufacturers also pay it the compliment of trying (not always successfully) to duplicate its good design. Usually, however, they are not quite deep enough and sometimes use unsuitable materials. Stainless steel, for instance, a notoriously bad conductor of heat, may make a good-looking wok but not a good cooking one. And though food might not stick in some non-stick woks, it scorches all too readily.

The original wok is such a sensible utensil. It has no corners to catch and burn; the high sides make it easy to toss and stir food without leaving a mess over the stove; and it requires very little oil when frying, because of its shape. It is ideal for stir-frying (a marvellously quick way of cooking — often taking less than 5 minutes actual cooking time), but remember to have all your ingredients ready — sliced, diced, chopped and measured — before you turn on the heat. Stir-frying is easy if you keep your mind on what you are doing and toss the ingredients in at the precise moment.

The wok can also be used for steaming, braising, simmering, stewing or frying. Then there is cross-cooking, where more than one method is used in the same recipe. Steaming is traditionally done in a bamboo steamer, but you can improvise by putting a trivet in the wok on which to rest the dish containing food. Use a cover that makes contact with the side of the wok so steam doesn't escape. Woks aren't usually sold with covers, but you'll find suitable covers in the same stores. A high domed cover is most versatile.

In Asia, woks are used mostly over fuel stoves, often just a clay bowl with fire in it. In western kitchens, gas is ideal for wok cooking, but if your cooking area does not have gas laid on, it is possible to buy wok burners which use bottled LP gas. These are a worthwhile investment if you frequently stir-fry and are great for outdoor cooking too.

If all you have is an electric hotplate, buy a wok made in heavier metal with a flattened base so it makes better contact with the heat. And because electric hotplates take some time to heat up and cool down, you must cook on highest heat and lift the wok off the hotplate when the cooking is done. Try working with two hotplates — one set to maximum and one on medium low. It involves a little to- and fro-ing but affords better control.

Electric woks are handsome and preferable to using a wok on an electric hotplate, but the heat is slow to build up. Remember, for best results, cook only small amounts of food at a time.

Choosing a Wok

The most reasonably priced woks are of rolled steel, which conducts heat well. They have the disadvantage, however, of rusting if not used frequently and dried scrupulously after use. They also have to be seasoned before use as described below.

The only other woks I recommend are enamel-coated woks. They never rust and will not impart a metallic flavour or greyish colour to any food left in them. If you use an ordinary steel wok, remember to remove the food to a dish as soon as it is cooked.

A rolled steel wok is usually coated with oil to prevent it rusting between factory and consumer. Sometimes this coating will come off with a good scrub in hot soapy water, but often it is stubborn and needs to be softened first. Do this by filling the wok with water, adding 2 or 3 tablespoons of bicarbonate of soda (baking soda) and boiling for 15 minutes. The coating can then be removed with a fine scourer. If necessary, repeat the process until there is no coating left on the inside. (Never mind the outside, it will burn off as you use the wok.)

Seasoning Your Steel Wok

This must be done after cleaning the protective coating off a new wok and before cooking in it. It is also the procedure for woks that have been allowed to rust or have had the smooth cooking surface destroyed when scoured with abrasive materials.

Dry the wok well and put it over gentle heat. When the metal is hot, wipe over the entire inner surface with a wad of absorbent kitchen paper dipped in peanut oil. Repeat a number of times, using fresh paper each time. At first the paper will come away a rusty brown, but after a few times it will remain clean. The wok is then ready for use.

After cooking, do not scrub with steel wool or abrasives or you will have to season it all over again. Soak in hot, soapy water to soften any food which sticks, then rub gently with a sponge. Dry the wok well and, before putting it away, heat it to make sure it is quite dry; the tiniest amount of moisture will cause it to rust. The best insurance against rust, however, is to use your wok often. A well-seasoned wok develops a shiny black cooking surface, which is quite normal and makes it even better to cook in. If you don't use the wok frequently, rub over the cooking surface with paper dipped in oil before putting it away.

Some people prefer a wok with a single handle, but personally I find it heavy to lift with one hand and prefer the traditional two-handled wok. But do remember to use a pot holder before grabbing the metal handles.

Successful Stir-frying

As this book is about what a wok does best, you will find I have concentrated on stir-frying. What is stir-frying? In western cooking, stirring implies a circular motion. If you have ever watched an oriental cook at work, you know that the action is more like tossing, flipping, keeping food constantly on the move so that all of it comes in contact with the hot wok.

Because the cooking takes just a few minutes once started, it is important to have all the ingredients ready or the whole performance will be spoilt. There can be no rushing to find something which should be added during the split-second timing. Have meat and vegetables sliced, garlic crushed, ginger grated, sauces and stock measured and ready. Arrange everything on a tray within reach, preferably in the correct order for adding to the wok. Run through the recipe in your mind before heating the wok. There is no time for checking a recipe once the action starts!

Speed and convenience aside, there is another advantage. Stir-frying requires very little oil, resulting in delicious, healthy, easy-to-digest meals.

The wok is ideal for cooking vegetables. Whether steaming, stir-frying or braising, all the goodness is kept and not poured away with the cooking water. The natural sweetness and crunchy texture achieved by short cooking appeals to all tastes.

Tossing vegetables in a small amount of oil for only a minute or two when stir-frying intensifies their colours — besides being an easy way to add flavour. Long cooking only lessens valuable vitamin content.

Even traditional salad vegetables, such as iceberg lettuce, can be transformed into a tantalising winter dish in one minute.

honey -glazed mushrooms

STIR-FRY, **serves 4**

300 g (10 oz) button mushrooms
1 tablespoon peanut oil
1 tablespoon honey
1 tablespoon soy sauce
1 teaspoon oriental sesame oil

Wipe mushrooms with damp paper towel and trim stalks. Heat oil in a wok, add mushrooms and stir-fry for 1 minute over medium heat. Stir in honey and soy sauce, lower heat and cover. Simmer for 3 minutes. Uncover and cook until liquid reduces and thickens, stirring to coat mushrooms in glaze. Turn off heat, sprinkle with sesame oil and mix. Serve hot or cold as an accompaniment to Chinese-style dishes.

cloud ears in hoi sin sauce

Dried wood fungus (also known as cloud ear, mouse ear, wood ear, jelly mushroom or black fungus) comes in small or large sizes. I have used the large variety, about 7 cm across in dried form; they swell to many times that size when soaked. If you use the smaller variety (about 1 cm across), use $^1/_2$ cup dry measure.

STIR-FRY, **serves 4**

- 6–8 pieces dried wood fungus
- 2 teaspoons hoi sin sauce
- 2 tablespoons light soy sauce
- 2 teaspoons peanut oil
- $^1/_2$ teaspoon crushed garlic
- 2 cups gai larn (Chinese broccoli) in bite-size pieces
- 1 teaspoon cornflour
- 1 teaspoon oriental sesame oil

Rinse wood fungus. Place in large bowl and cover generously with hot water. Soak 10 minutes. Fungus will more than double in size. Drain and cut into bite-size pieces, discarding tough, gritty parts. Mix hoi sin and soy sauces with $^1/_4$ cup water. Heat peanut oil and fry garlic and gai larn for a few seconds, add sauce mixture and wood fungus and stir until mixture boils. Mix cornflour with 2 tablespoons cold water, add to wok and cook until liquid thickens. Stir in sesame oil and serve immediately with rice or noodles.

chinese

stir-fried vegetables

1 cup cauliflower florets
1 cup broccoli florets
2 carrots, thinly sliced
125 g (4 oz) snow peas or sugar
  snap peas
1 red capsicum
250 g (8 oz) mushrooms

2 tablespoons peanut oil
2 cloves garlic, crushed
1 teaspoon finely grated fresh
  ginger
2 tablespoons light soy sauce
$1/2$ cup vegetable stock
2 teaspoons cornflour

Blanch cauliflower, broccoli and carrot until tender but still crunchy. Reserve cooking liquid for vegetable stock. Wash and string peas and cut capsicum into thin strips. Trim stems off mushrooms, cutting caps into thick slices.

Heat oil in wok and stir-fry garlic and ginger for 30 seconds. Add peas, capsicum and mushrooms and stir-fry on high heat for 1 minute. Stir in soy sauce and vegetable stock. Add cornflour mixed with 2 tablespoons cold water and stir until liquid clears and thickens. Toss in blanched vegetables and heat through. Serve immediately with steamed rice.

heavenly braised vegetables

10 dried shiitake (Chinese)
   mushrooms
4 large pieces dried wood fungus
1 tablespoon peanut oil
1 tablespoon oriental sesame oil
1 cup sliced canned winter
   bamboo shoot

1 x 440 g (15 oz) can young corn
   cobs, drained or fresh baby
   corn
1 tablespoon soy sauce
1 tablespoon oyster sauce
1 tablespoon sugar

Soak mushrooms in hot water to cover for 30 minutes. Discard stems, squeeze moisture from caps and cut in halves, quarters if large. Reserve soaking liquid. Soak wood fungus in fresh cold water for 20 minutes. Drain and cut into bite-size pieces. Discard gritty bits.

Heat oils in wok and brown mushrooms. Add 2 cups reserved mushroom liquid and remaining ingredients, except for wood fungus. Reduce heat and simmer, covered, for 25 minutes or until mushrooms are tender and liquid is reduced and syrupy.

Add wood fungus and simmer 5 minutes longer. Serve with rice.

szechwan -style eggplant

A robust dish. Serve cold as an hors d'oeuvre or hot with rice.

DEEP-FRY, **serves 6–8**

1 kg (2 lb) eggplants
2 cups peanut oil
2 teaspoons finely grated ginger
2 teaspoons finely chopped garlic
1 red capsicum, cut in large
   squares
6 spring onions, sliced diagonally

Sauce
$^1/_2$ cup dark soy sauce
$^1/_4$ cup Chinese black vinegar or
   cider vinegar
1 tablespoon dry sherry
1 tablespoon sugar
2 teaspoons oriental sesame oil
2 teaspoons sweet chilli sauce

Wash and dry eggplants. Do not peel. Cut into large cubes and fry small amounts in hot oil till golden brown, removing with a slotted spoon. Pour off oil, leaving 1 tablespoon.

Mix ingredients for sauce, stirring to dissolve sugar. Reheat oil and fry ginger, garlic, capsicum and spring onions on low heat until garlic is golden. Add sauce and boil. Add eggplant and toss until most of the sauce is absorbed.

eggplant with spicy sauce

Eggplant is especially delicious when fried, but it does soak up oil! Try steaming or boiling instead, adding spiciness with this sauce.

STEAM/STIR-FRY, **serves 6**

750 g (1¹/₂ lb) firm eggplants
2 tablespoons peanut oil
1 teaspoon dried shrimp paste
5 brazil nuts, finely grated
1 teaspoon finely chopped
   galangal in brine or laos powder

1 fresh red chilli, finely chopped
2 tablespoons dark soy sauce
2 teaspoons palm sugar or brown
   sugar
¹/₂ cup canned coconut milk
1 tablespoon tamarind extract

Peel eggplant and dice. Place in a steamer and steam over boiling water until tender. Drain.

Heat wok, add oil and fry shrimp paste over low heat, stirring constantly and mashing with back of cooking spoon. Add grated nuts and fry, stirring, for 1 minute. Add galangal, chilli, soy sauce, sugar, coconut milk and tamarind extract dissolved in ¹/₄ cup hot water. Stir and simmer gently until heated through. Pour over eggplant and serve with rice.

stir-fried asparagus and capsicum, thai style

I love the colours of brilliant green asparagus and bright red capsicums in this quick and delicious dish.

STIR-FRY, **serves 6-8**

500 g (1 lb) asparagus
2 red capsicums
**2 teaspoons green peppercorns,
  fresh or brined**
2 teaspoons finely chopped garlic
2 tablespoons fish sauce
2 tablespoons Maggi Seasoning
1 tablespoon sugar
2 red chillies, sliced (optional)
3 tablespoons peanut oil

Wash vegetables and dry on paper towels. Snap off tough ends of asparagus and cut spears into bite-size lengths. Cut capsicum into strips of similar size. Crush peppercorns. Combine garlic, peppercorns, sauces, sugar and chilli. Stir until sugar dissolves.

Heat oil in wok and stir-fry vegetables on high heat until colours intensify. Add ¼ cup water, cover and steam for 2 to 3 minutes until vegetables are tender but still crisp. Add combined seasonings, stir until sauce boils and serve immediately with rice.

tofu
in hot sauce

So you thought bean curd was bland? Try this dish and think again.

SIMMER, **serves 4**

500 g (1 lb) fresh soft bean curd
1 tablespoon peanut oil
1 teaspoon finely chopped ginger
1 clove garlic, finely chopped
1 teaspoon chilli bean paste
1 tablespoon tomato sauce

salt to taste
1 teaspoon sugar
1 teaspoon dark soy sauce
2 teaspoons cornflour
3 spring onions, sliced diagonally

Cut bean curd into 1 cm ($^1/_2$ in) cubes. Bring 4 cups water to boil in wok, add bean curd and simmer gently until heated through. Remove with strainer and leave to drain. Dry wok, heat oil and stir-fry ginger and garlic until fragrant. Add $^1/_2$ cup water and remaining ingredients, except spring onions and cornflour, and bring to boil. Blend cornflour with 1 tablespoon water, stir into sauce and cook, stirring, for a couple of minutes until clear and thick. Add spring onions and warm bean curd to sauce and toss gently to coat. Serve immediately with steamed rice.

bean curd with peanuts

A high-protein vegetarian main dish to serve with rice or on its own.

DEEP-FRY, **serves 4**

500 g (1 lb) firm bean curd
  peanut oil for frying
$^1/_3$ cup raw peanuts
1 teaspoon crushed garlic
$^1/_2$ teaspoon dried shrimp paste
$^1/_2$ cup crunchy peanut butter
2 tablespoons ketjap manis
  (sweetened dark soy)

$^1/_2$ teaspoon sambal ulek
1 teaspoon palm sugar or
  brown sugar
3 tablespoons vinegar
$^1/_3$ cup canned coconut milk
1 cup shredded cabbage
1 cup fresh bean sprouts
3 spring onions, finely sliced

Place bean curd between paper towels, pressing gently to dry. This will minimise spattering when frying. Cut into small dice. In hot oil, fry bean curd until golden. Lift out and drain on paper towels. Fry peanuts for 3 to 4 minutes; lift out on slotted spoon and drain on paper until cool enough to rub off skins.

Pour off all but 1 tablespoon of oil and fry garlic and shrimp paste over low heat, stirring and mashing with back of spoon. Add peanut butter, ketjap manis, sambal ulek, sugar and vinegar. Remove from heat. Gradually stir in coconut milk until sauce is of a thick pouring consistency.

Place bean curd on serving dish and spoon sauce over. Scatter cabbage and bean sprouts over and garnish with spring onions and fried peanuts.

vegetables indonesian style

750 g (1¹/₂ lb) mixed seasonal
  vegetables (cauliflower,
  broccoli, beans, cabbage,
  zucchini, pumpkin, etc.)
2 tablespoons peanut oil
2 onions, finely chopped
2 teaspoons crushed garlic
1 teaspoon chopped red chilli
  or sambal ulek
1 teaspoon dried shrimp paste

1 stalk lemon grass or 2 strips
  lemon rind, finely chopped
1 large ripe tomato, peeled,
  seeded and chopped
2 cups chicken stock
1 cup canned coconut milk
1 tablespoon peanut butter
2 teaspoons ketjap manis
  (sweetened dark soy)
  lemon juice, optional

Cut vegetables into small pieces: cauliflower or broccoli in sprigs, beans sliced diagonally, cabbage roughly shredded then cut crosswise, zucchini and pumpkin sliced or diced. Heat oil in wok and stir-fry onion until soft and golden. Add garlic, chilli and shrimp paste and fry on low heat for 2 minutes, crushing shrimp paste with back of spoon. Add lemon grass or rind and tomato. Cook, stirring, until reduced. Add stock and coconut milk and bring to simmer, uncovered. Add vegetables, putting those which require longer cooking in first, and toss until tender but still crisp. Stir in peanut butter and ketjap manis. Add a squeeze of lemon juice for extra tang.

Whichever method of cooking you use, the secret with seafood is not to overcook it.

As soon as fish turns opaque, it is done. Prawns lose their translucent appearance and become pink and white. Squid turns white and curls. Scallops become white and opaque.

The smaller sea creatures take just seconds to cook in the high heat of a wok — any longer and they will be tough and chewy.

So, remember the golden rule of wok cooking — have all ingredients ready so the rhythm of the cooking is not interrupted.

stir-fried prawns with lychees

STIR-FRY, **serves 4-6**

750 g (1¹/₂ lb) medium-size
raw prawns
1 teaspoon cornflour
¹/₂ teaspoon salt
1 tablespoon egg white
¹/₂ teaspoon finely grated ginger
1 red capsicum
24 fresh or canned lychees
2 tablespoons peanut oil

Sauce
2 teaspoons tomato paste
2 tablespoons rice vinegar or
white wine vinegar
1 teaspoon cornflour
1 teaspoon sugar
salt to taste

Shell prawns, leaving tail on. Remove vein and slit prawns almost through on back curve.

Rinse in cold water and dry on paper towels. Mix prawns with cornflour, salt, egg white and ginger, cover and chill 30 minutes. Cut capsicum into squares, discarding seeds and membrane. Peel and seed fresh lychees or, if canned, drain well. Combine sauce ingredients with ¹/₄ cup water, stirring until sugar dissolves.

Heat 1 tablespoon oil in wok and stir-fry prawns, tossing until they turn pink and start to

curl. Remove from wok. Wash out wok, add remaining oil and stir-fry capsicum for 1 minute. Return prawns to wok, add lychees and sauce, stirring constantly, until sauce thickens. Serve immediately with hot rice.

crystal prawns with green vegetables

BOIL/STIR-FRY, **serves 4**

16 large raw prawns
salt
1 egg white, beaten slightly
3 teaspoons cornflour
1 head firm, fresh broccoli or
    1 bundle tender asparagus
1 tablespoon peanut oil
$1/2$ teaspoon finely grated
    fresh ginger

1 small clove garlic, crushed
1 tablespoon dry sherry
2 teaspoons cornflour
2 tablespoons shredded red
    ginger in syrup
green part of 1 spring onion,
    finely sliced

Shell and devein prawns, leaving tail on. In a bowl, sprinkle prawns with 1 teaspoon salt and stir vigorously with a wooden spoon or with chopsticks, for 1 full minute. Rinse in a colander under cold running water for 1 minute. Repeat twice more, using a teaspoon of salt each time and beating prawns well. (This ensures a crisp texture when cooked.) After final rinsing, dry on kitchen towels. With point of a sharp knife make a small slit through underside of prawns. Return to bowl and add egg white, $1/2$ teaspoon salt and 3 teaspoons cornflour. Mix to thoroughly coat prawns. Cover and chill for 1 hour.

Cut broccoli into florets, leaving about 5 cm (2 in) of green stem on each piece. Push end of stem through slit in prawn so that floret rests within curve. If using asparagus, snap off tough ends and pass spear through prawn. Reserve any extra vegetable. Half fill a wok with water and when boiling, drop in prawns and vegetable. Stir. As soon as prawns become pink and vegetable a brilliant green, drain in colander.

Dry wok, add oil and fry fresh ginger and garlic for a few seconds. Add dry sherry and $1/3$ cup water. Add cornflour mixed with 1 tablespoon cold water to wok and stir until sauce thickens. Drop prawns and vegetables in and toss lightly to coat. Serve at once, garnished with shredded red ginger and spring onion slices. Accompany with hot white rice.

eggs foo yong with prawns

SHALLOW-FRY, **serves 4**

250 g (8 oz) cooked prawns
6 eggs
$1/2$ teaspoon salt
$1/4$ teaspoon ground black pepper
6 spring onions, finely chopped
peanut oil for frying
2 tablespoons chopped coriander
leaves for garnish

Sauce
1 tablespoon light soy sauce
4 tablespoons dry sherry
2 tablespoons rice vinegar or
white wine vinegar
2 tablespoons white sugar
1 tablespoon cornflour
1 tablespoon shredded red ginger

Shell, devein and roughly chop prawns. Beat eggs with salt and pepper. Mix in prawns and spring onions.

Heat wok, add 2 teaspoons oil and swirl to coat centre. Pour in 2 tablespoons egg mixture. When browned on underside, turn and cook other side. Transfer to a plate and keep warm. Repeat until remaining mixture is used up.

Wipe out wok with kitchen paper. Combine soy sauce, sherry, vinegar, sugar and $3/4$ cup water in wok and stir over medium heat until sugar dissolves. Bring to boil. Blend cornflour with 2 tablespoons cold water, stir into sauce and cook, stirring constantly, until thickened. Add red ginger and mix through. Serve with sauce and a sprinkling of coriander leaves.

prawns with chilli

STIR-FRY, **serves 4**

750 g (1^1/$_2$ lb) raw prawns
2 fresh red chillies
1 fresh green chilli
1 clove garlic
1 tablespoon sugar
2 teaspoons finely grated
fresh ginger

2 tablespoons light soy sauce
2 tablespoons dry sherry
3 tablespoons peanut oil
3 spring onions, sliced

Shell and devein prawns, then rinse and dry on paper towels. Seed chillies and slice finely.

Crush garlic with a teaspoon of the sugar and mix with chillies and ginger. Stir remaining sugar with soy sauce and sherry, until sugar dissolves.

Heat oil in wok and stir-fry prawns until colour changes. Remove to a plate. In remaining oil fry chillies, garlic and ginger, stirring, until garlic is golden. Stir in sauce mixture. When hot add prawns and stir until heated through. Sprinkle with spring onion and serve at once with hot rice or noodles.

stir-fried scallops with snow peas

STIR-FRY, **serves 2-3**

250 g (8 oz) scallops
4 spring onions
125 g (4 oz) snow peas or sugar
   snap peas
2 tablespoons peanut oil
1 teaspoon finely grated
   fresh ginger

1 clove garlic, finely chopped
2 teaspoons cornflour
2 teaspoons light soy sauce
   salt
   pinch of sugar
$1/2$ teaspoon oriental sesame oil

Clean scallops and dry on kitchen paper. Cut spring onions, white and green parts, into bite-size pieces. String snow peas.

Heat peanut oil in wok and stir-fry peas for 1 minute. Add spring onions, ginger and garlic, stir-fry 15 seconds. Remove to a plate. Mix cornflour with soy sauce and $1/2$ cup water. Pour into wok and cook, stirring, until thickened, about 1 minute. Add scallops and simmer for 1 minute, just until they begin to turn opaque. Stir in vegetables. Season to taste with salt and a pinch of sugar, stir in sesame oil and serve immediately with hot rice.

quick-boiled sizzling fish

Most wok enthusiasts have more than one wok. Here is a recipe where you can use two for best results.

BOIL/FRY, **serves 4**

1 whole white fish, about
  1 kg (2 lb)
salt
1 onion, peeled and sliced
  few celery tops
8 slices fresh ginger
20 whole black peppercorns

1 tablespoon chicken
  stock powder
3 tablespoons peanut oil
½ cup finely diced fat bacon
1 tablespoon dark soy sauce
2 teaspoons oriental sesame oil
  spring onions for garnish

Buy fish cleaned and scaled. Scrub cavity with damp paper towel dipped in coarse salt to remove all traces of blood. Trim spines with sharp scissors.

Three-quarter fill wok with water and add onion, celery, ginger, peppercorns and chicken stock powder. Bring to boil and simmer 6 to 8 minutes so liquid develops flavour. Gently slide fish into the water and return to boil. Lower heat and poach gently for 8 minutes or until flesh is opaque when tested. Lift out on wire spoon or two large fish slices, let excess liquid drain for a few seconds, and carefully place fish on a large platter.

While fish is cooking, heat oil in another wok and fry bacon until crisp, stirring. Mix soy sauce and sesame oil and pour over fish, then pour the sizzling hot oil and fried bacon over and serve at once.

Note Don't waste the stock in which the fish was cooked. Strain and cook some thin slices of winter melon or other Chinese vegetable in it for a few minutes and serve as soup.

spicy fried fish

One of the advantages of wok cooking is that, even when deep-frying, not much oil is needed because of the shape of the utensil.

DEEP-FRY, **serves 4**

8 dried shiitake
  (Chinese) mushrooms
750 g (1¹/₂ lb) fish fillets
¹/₂ cup cornflour
¹/₂ teaspoon salt
¹/₂ teaspoon five spice powder
  peanut oil for frying

Sauce
1 tablespoon peanut oil
3 spring onions, sliced
1 clove garlic, finely chopped
2 tablespoons light soy sauce
¹/₂ teaspoon five spice powder
1 tablespoon sugar
1 scant teaspoon chilli bean sauce
2 teaspoons cornflour
  spring onion curls (see Note)

Soak mushrooms in hot water for 30 minutes. Squeeze excess water from mushrooms (reserve soaking water), discard stems and cut caps into halves or quarters. Slice fish into strips and dip in cornflour mixed with salt and five spice powder. Heat ¹/₂ cup oil in wok until a haze rises from surface. Add half the fish at a time and deep-fry for 2 minutes. Drain on absorbent paper and transfer to serving dish. Keep warm. Discard frying oil.

Wipe out wok with kitchen paper. Heat 1 tablespoon oil and stir-fry mushrooms, spring onions and garlic. Stir in soy sauce, five spice powder, sugar, chilli bean sauce and 1 cup of the mushroom soaking liquid. Simmer for 10 minutes. Add cornflour blended with 1 tablespoon water and bring to boil, stirring. Pour over fish. Garnish with spring onions and serve with hot white rice.

Note   To make spring onion curls, slit green portions several times with a pin and drop into iced water for 5 to 10 minutes.

fried
fish with crab sauce

DEEP-FRY, **serves 4**

750 g (1¹/₂ lb) white fish fillets
¹/₂ teaspoon finely grated
fresh ginger
1 clove garlic, crushed
salt to taste
cornflour for coating fish
peanut oil for deep-frying

Crab Sauce
2 tablespoons peanut oil
4 spring onions, chopped,
including green part
1 teaspoon finely grated ginger
1 cup chicken stock
185 g (6 oz) crab meat
pinch of sugar and salt to taste
3 teaspoons cornflour

Remove skin from fish, wash and dry with paper towels. Rub fish with ginger, garlic and salt. Cut into bite-sized pieces and toss in cornflour. Heat oil in wok and quickly fry fish over medium heat, a few pieces at a time, for about 1 minute. Drain on paper towels, transfer to serving dish and keep warm.

Discard oil and wipe over wok. Heat 2 tablespoons peanut oil and fry spring onions and ginger for a few seconds over low heat, stirring constantly. Add stock, cover and simmer for 3 to 4 minutes. Add crab meat, heat for 1 minute. Adjust seasoning with sugar and salt. Blend cornflour with 2 tablespoons cold water and stir into sauce until it boils and thickens. Spoon sauce over fish and serve immediately.

chilli squid

The key to success of this or any other squid dish is the very short cooking time.

DEEP-FRY/STIR-FRY,
serves 4-6

750 g (1½ lb) cleaned squid
½ teaspoon salt
1 egg white
1 tablespoon cornflour
1 tablespoon peanut oil
1 medium-sized red chilli
1 medium-sized green chilli
1 clove garlic

6 spring onions
1 teaspoon sugar
1 teaspoon chilli oil
2 teaspoons cornflour
peanut oil for frying
125 g (4 oz) snow peas or sugar
snap peas

Slit squid with a sharp knife and score cleaned inner surface with parallel cuts 6 mm (¼ in) apart to make a pattern of small diamonds. Cut into pieces 5 cm (2 in) square. Mix squid with salt, egg white, cornflour and peanut oil. Cover and chill for at least 30 minutes.

Seed chillies and cut into thin slices. Chop garlic finely and cut spring onions diagonally into bite-sized lengths. Mix sugar, chilli oil and salt to taste into ½ cup water. Blend cornflour with 2 tablespoons cold water.

Heat 1½ cups peanut oil in wok and when hot add half the squid and fry on high heat about 1 minute, just until squid curls. Scoop from wok at once with a large perforated spoon. Repeat with remaining squid. Pour oil into a heatproof bowl. It may be strained and used again. Return wok to heat with just a film of oil and stir-fry snow peas for 1 minute. Add garlic, chillies and spring onions and stir-fry over high heat for 1 minute.

Add sugar and chilli oil mixture and as soon as it boils stir in cornflour mixture until it thickens. Return drained squid and heat through — do not boil. Garnish with a chilli flower and serve with steamed rice.

lobster with ginger

FRY/BRAISE, **serves 2**

2 green lobster tails
1 egg white, slightly beaten
1 tablespoon cornflour
3 cups peanut oil
2 tablespoons finely shredded
   fresh ginger
$^1/_2$ cup sliced spring onions, the
   pieces should be 5 cm (2 in)
   long
1 cup hot chicken stock
3 teaspoons cornflour

Chop lobster tails into pieces, coat with egg white, cornflour and 1 tablespoon peanut oil.

Chill 30 minutes. Heat oil (saving 1 tablespoon) and deep-fry lobster until shell turns red and meat becomes white. Pour lobster and oil into a wire colander over a heat-proof bowl.

Return wok to heat with remaining oil, stir-fry ginger and spring onion for

10 seconds, return lobster. Add stock, cover and steam on high heat for 2 minutes. Stir in cornflour mixed with 1 tablespoon cold water until sauce boils and thickens. Serve at once.

With the accent on speedy cooking, for most of these recipes you can do no better than buy chicken already filleted and free of skin.

In some recipes, however, flavour will be lost if the chicken is not cut the Asian way — not just jointed, but cut with a cleaver through the bones. The marrow and juices from the bones add to the taste and the pieces are small enough for all the flavours to penetrate. The bite-sized morsels are easily managed with chopsticks and bones are politely discarded on the bone plate, which is part of the Chinese place setting. (Provide saucers if you don't have bone plates.)

Use quick, decisive movements for chopping through bones and make sure the cleaver is sharp and has a suitably thick blade — a fine knife would be ruined. Take care not to overcook chicken, especially breast fillets. Diced chicken is cooked in a minute or less over a high gas flame; over an electric hotplate it takes a little longer, but watch carefully — it is cooked as soon as it turns white.

chicken
with corn and cashews

1.5 kg (3 lb) assorted chicken pieces
1 teaspoon salt or to taste
$1/2$ teaspoon five spice powder
$1/2$ cup peanut oil
1 cup raw cashews
2 teaspoons finely grated
   fresh ginger

2 cloves garlic, crushed
$1/2$ cup chicken stock
1 tablespoon light soy sauce
1 teaspoon sugar
3 teaspoons cornflour
1 x 425 g (15 oz) can baby corn
   cobs, drained

Chop chicken into bite-sized pieces, wipe over with paper towel to remove any fragments of bone. Rub chicken with salt and five spice powder. Place in heatproof dish on steaming rack or trivet in wok with water to just below rack. Cover and steam 15 minutes, or until cooked. (Reserve any liquid that collects in dish and add to stock.)

Dry wok thoroughly. Add peanut oil and heat. Fry cashews over medium heat, stirring constantly, until golden brown. Remove with slotted spoon and drain on paper towels. Pour off all but 1 tablespoon oil from wok. Lower heat and fry ginger and garlic, stirring constantly, for a few seconds until they begin to colour. Add chicken stock, soy sauce and sugar. Blend cornflour with 1 tablespoon cold water. Bring mixture in wok to a brisk boil, stir in cornflour until sauce thickens, add corn and return to boil. Pour over chicken, scatter cashews over and serve with rice.

braised
chicken with fresh mushrooms

If you are able to obtain different varieties of fresh mushrooms, such as shiitake or oyster (abalone) mushrooms, combine them with cultivated mushrooms.

BRAISE, **serves 4**

500 g (1 lb) fresh mushrooms
500 g (1 lb) chicken thigh fillets
3 tablespoons peanut oil
**1 teaspoon finely chopped
  fresh ginger**
1 teaspoon finely chopped garlic
2 tablespoons dark soy sauce
2 teaspoons chilli sauce
1 teaspoon oriental sesame oil

Wipe mushrooms with damp paper towel. Don't wash, as they absorb water. Trim stems and, if mushrooms are large, cut into pieces. Cut chicken into bite-sized pieces.

Heat peanut oil in wok and fry ginger and garlic, stirring, until golden. Add chicken and stir-fry for 2 minutes over high heat. Stir in 1/2 cup water, soy sauce, chilli sauce and mushrooms. Cover and simmer for 10 minutes. Raise heat and cook, uncovered, until most of the liquid has evaporated. Add sesame oil, toss and serve with rice.

chicken with snow peas

STIR-FRY, **serves 4**

500 g (1 lb) chicken breast fillets
1 clove garlic, crushed
$^1/_2$ teaspoon finely grated
fresh ginger
1 tablespoon light soy sauce
1 tablespoon dry sherry

125 g (4 oz) snow peas or sugar
snap peas
2 tablespoons peanut oil
4 tablespoons chicken stock
or water
1 teaspoon cornflour

Cut chicken in very thin slices, mix with garlic, ginger, half the soy and half the sherry.

String snow peas, drop into lightly salted boiling water. As soon as water returns to boil, drain and refresh peas in iced water to keep colour bright and texture crisp.

Heat oil in wok and stir-fry chicken until it turns white. Add remaining soy, sherry and stock or water; simmer for 2 minutes. Blend cornflour with 1 tablespoon cold water and stir in until sauce thickens. Add snow peas and toss gently. Serve immediately with hot rice.

chicken with ginger

A Thai dish usually made with chicken on the bone, chopped through in the Asian manner into bite-sized pieces. For even quicker preparation and cooking, use convenient fillets.

STIR-FRY, **serves 4**

500 g (1 lb) chicken thigh fillets or
half a roasting chicken
2 tablespoons peanut oil
3 cloves garlic, crushed
2 tablespoons fish sauce
1 tablespoon vinegar
1 teaspoon dark soy sauce

2 teaspoons palm sugar
2 tablespoons finely shredded
fresh ginger
1 teaspoon cornflour
few sprigs fresh mint leaves
torn in pieces

Cut chicken into bite-sized pieces. Heat oil and fry garlic for 10 seconds, then add chicken and stir-fry until all chicken is golden. Add fish sauce, vinegar, soy sauce, palm sugar, ginger and $1/4$ cup water, cover and simmer for 3 minutes if using chicken fillets or, if chicken on the bone, until flesh near bone is no longer pink. Add cornflour blended with 1 tablespoon cold water and stir until thickened. Sprinkle with mint and serve with steamed rice.

stir-fried chicken and capsicums

The red, white and green of this dish are pleasingly colourful.

STIR-FRY, **serves 4**

375 g (12 oz) chicken breast fillets
1/2 teaspoon salt
1 tablespoon egg white
2 teaspoons cornflour
3 tablespoons peanut oil
1 red capsicum
1 green capsicum

1 teaspoon finely grated
  fresh ginger
2 cloves garlic, crushed
1/2 cup chicken stock
1 tablespoon dry sherry
2 tablespoons light soy sauce
2 teaspoons cornflour

Cut chicken into bite-sized pieces. Add salt, egg white, cornflour and 1 tablespoon of oil and mix well. Cover and chill for about 30 minutes. Core capsicums and cut into even-size squares or strips, discarding seeds.

Heat wok, add 1 tablespoon oil and stir-fry capsicums over high heat for 1 minute. Remove. Add remaining oil and fry ginger and garlic for a few seconds; add chicken and stir-fry for 1 to 2 minutes over high heat.

Mix chicken stock, sherry, soy sauce and cornflour together, pour into wok and stir until it boils and thickens.

Return capsicums to wok and heat through. Transfer to serving dish and serve with rice.

the colonel's
chicken

No, not that colonel, but one who spent his working life in India and enjoyed the household cook's version of a western pot roast.

BRAISE, **serves 6**

1.5 kg (3 lb) chicken or
  chicken pieces
2 cloves garlic, crushed
  salt to taste
1 teaspoon ground turmeric
1/2 teaspoon ground black pepper

4 tablespoons peanut oil
4 large onions, very thinly sliced
2 fresh red chillies, seeded
  and sliced
1 teaspoon garam masala
  (see p.88)

Joint chicken. Mix garlic, salt, turmeric and pepper and rub well into chicken. Leave for 30 minutes. Heat oil in wok and gently fry half the onions, stirring frequently, until brown. Remove onion from wok with slotted spoon and set aside.

Add a tablespoon more oil and stir-fry remaining onion and chillies until just starting to colour. Add chicken and fry over high heat until golden all over. Add 1/2 cup water, sprinkle with garam masala, cover and simmer, stirring occasionally, until tender, adding a little water if necessary. Uncover and cook quickly to reduce liquid. Serve hot, garnished with reserved fried onion and accompanied by rice or potatoes.

chicken
with peanut sauce

BRAISE, serves 6-8

1.5 kg (3 lb) chicken thigh fillets
2 tablespoons peanut oil
2 tablespoons Red Curry Paste
   (see below)
2 teaspoons finely chopped garlic
2 teaspoons finely chopped
   fresh ginger

1 cup canned coconut milk
2 tablespoons crunchy
   peanut butter
1 rounded teaspoon palm or
   brown sugar
2 tablespoons fish sauce

Cut thigh fillets into 2 or 3 pieces. Heat oil and fry Red Curry Paste, garlic and ginger over low heat, stirring constantly, until mixture smells beautifully fragrant. Add chicken and fry, turning to coat with curry paste. Add coconut milk mixed with 1 cup water and when boiling stir in peanut butter, palm sugar and fish sauce. Simmer, uncovered, until flavours mellow and chicken is cooked. Serve with freshly cooked rice.

red curry paste

6 to 8 fresh red chillies
2 small brown onions, chopped
1 teaspoon black peppercorns
2 teaspoons ground cummin
1 tablespoon ground coriander
2 tablespoons chopped fresh
   coriander, including root
1 teaspoon salt
1 tablespoon chopped garlic

1 stem lemon grass, finely sliced
   or 2 teaspoons chopped
   lemon rind
2 teaspoons chopped galangal
   in brine
2 teaspoons dried shrimp paste
1 teaspoon turmeric
2 teaspoons paprika (see Note)

Remove stems from chillies (if you want the curry to be as hot as it is in Thailand, leave seeds in). Cut chillies into pieces, then place in electric blender with all other ingredients. Blend to a smooth paste, stopping frequently to push ingredients down with a spatula. You may need a little extra water, to assist with blending. Store in refrigerator in tightly sealed glass jar for a month or more.

Note While paprika is not used in Thailand, I have added it to give the requisite red colour without too many red chillies.

braised honey chicken

Children love this combination of flavours, and it makes great finger food for parties or picnics.

BRAISE, serves 4-6

1 kg (2 lb) chicken wings
2 tablespoons peanut oil
$1/_2$ cup dark soy sauce
2 tablespoons honey
1 star anise (8 segments)
1 small clove garlic, finely
   chopped

3 tablespoons dry sherry
1 teaspoon finely chopped
   fresh ginger
2 tablespoons toasted sesame
   seeds, optional
2 spring onions

Divide chicken wings at joints and discard wing tips. Heat oil and brown chicken over high heat. Add remaining ingredients (except sesame seeds), stirring well to dissolve honey. Cover and simmer over gentle heat for 25 minutes or until chicken wings are tender. Stir towards end of cooking to ensure that honey does not burn. Serve at room temperature sprinkled with sesame seeds and garnished with spring onions.

braised
szechwan chicken

The inland province of Szechwan is renowned for its hot, spicy flavours – but the many dried chillies are only for those who enjoy picking them up and biting into them, the flavour does not make the whole dish pungent.

BRAISE, **serves 4-6**

1.5 kg (3 lb) chicken
1 teaspoon Szechwan peppercorns
1 teaspoon five spice powder
1 teaspoon salt
¹/₃ cup cornflour
¹/₂ cup chicken stock
2 teaspoons sugar
1 tablespoon soy sauce
1 teaspoon oriental sesame oil

1 teaspoon rice vinegar
2 tablespoons dry sherry
¹/₂ cup peanut oil for frying
12 dried red chillies, seeded
2 cloves garlic, finely chopped
2 teaspoons finely chopped
fresh ginger
4 spring onions, chopped in 5 cm
(2 in lengths)

Cut chicken into serving pieces, chopping through bones with a cleaver. Wipe over with damp kitchen paper to remove any fragments of bone. Reserve back and neck for stock. Discard tail and excess fat from cavity.

Toast Szechwan peppercorns in a dry pan until fragrant, then crush to powder. Mix with five spice powder, salt and cornflour (reserving 1 teaspoon for thickening). Toss chicken pieces in mixture. Dust off excess. Combine stock, sugar, soy sauce, sesame oil, vinegar and sherry.

Heat oil in wok and when very hot add one-third of the chicken pieces. Fry on high heat, tossing chicken to brown all over. Drain on paper towel. Repeat with remaining chicken, allowing oil to get hot again between batches. Pour off all but 2 tablespoons oil. Add chillies, garlic and ginger and fry for about 1 minute till garlic and ginger are golden and chillies darken. Add spring onions and toss for a few seconds, then add stock mixture and bring to boil. Return chicken to wok, cover and simmer until chicken is tender, about 20 minutes.

Mix reserved cornflour with 1 tablespoon cold water. Stir into sauce until it boils and thickens. Serve with hot white rice.

You can't cook a large slab of meat quickly, so sharpen your knives and be prepared to slice meat thinner than for any western recipe. To make it easy to cut meat in paper-thin slices, partially freeze it first to make it firm.

Because meat is cooked for only 3 or 4 minutes, it has to be good quality fillet or rump steak and these are not exactly cheap — but you don't have to break the budget. With forward planning you can use economy cuts such as round, blade or silverside. The cooking is just as quick, but first the meat has to be marinated for some hours with a tenderising mixture that is the secret of many Chinese restaurants.

Dissolve $\frac{1}{2}$ teaspoon bicarbonate of soda in 3 tablespoons hot water, pour over 500 g (1 lb) finely sliced meat and mix well until all the water is absorbed. Cover and refrigerate for at least 2 hours, preferably longer, then proceed with the recipe. The meat will be very tender.

stir-fried pork with cashews

STIR-FRY, serves 4

375 g (12 oz) lean, tender pork
1 medium onion
1 red or green capsicum (or half of each)
3 tablespoons peanut oil
1/2 cup raw cashews
1 clove garlic, finely chopped

1/2 teaspoon finely chopped fresh ginger
2 teaspoons light soy sauce
2 tablespoons dry sherry
1 teaspoon cornflour
1 spring onion, sliced diagonally into small pieces

Partially freeze pork to firm and cut in paper-thin slices. Peel onion, cut in quarters lengthwise and then in halves across. Separate layers. Cut capsicums to similar size and shape.

Heat oil and fry cashews until golden brown. Remove with slotted spoon and drain on paper towel. Add capsicum and onion and stir-fry on high heat for 1 minute. Remove to plate. In remaining oil stir-fry garlic and ginger for 30 seconds. Add pork and stir-fry until colour changes. Add soy sauce and sherry, cover and simmer for 2 minutes. Push pork to side of wok. Mix cornflour with 2 tablespoons cold water, add to wok and stir until sauce thickens. Return capsicum, onion and cashews, sprinkle with spring onion and serve at once.

stir-fried pork and three-colour vegetables

Because everything is cut finely, this is really quick to cook. Serve with rice for a well-balanced meal. Have the rice cooked and ready before starting to stir-fry.

STIR-FRY, serves 2

2 small carrots
2 small zucchini
1 stick celery
250 g (8 oz) pork fillet
1 tablespoon hoi sin sauce
2 teaspoons cornflour
1 tablespoon peanut oil
1 clove garlic, crushed
1 teaspoon finely chopped ginger

Peel carrots and trim ends of zucchini. Cut all vegetables into fine julienne strips and set aside. Slice pork paper-thin. Combine hoi sin sauce with $1/2$ cup water and cornflour.

Heat wok, add oil and stir-fry garlic and ginger over low heat for 30 seconds. Increase heat, add pork and stir fry, tossing, until browned. Add vegetables and stir-fry for about 2 minutes, until colour brightens and vegetables are tender but still crisp.

Push pork and vegetables to side of wok and pour hoi sin mixture into centre. Stir until sauce boils. Toss pork and vegetables through sauce.

stir-fried pork with noodles

Chilli bean sauce makes this a very zingy dish, but if your tastebuds are not attuned to chilli, simply leave it out.

STIR-FRY, **serves 4**

250 g (8 oz) lean, boneless pork
250 g (8 oz) egg noodles
3 tablespoons peanut oil
1 tablespoon dry sherry
2 tablespoons light soy sauce
1 red capsicum, sliced
2 cloves garlic, finely chopped

2 teaspoons finely chopped
  fresh ginger
2 teaspoons chilli bean sauce or
  to taste
2 fresh red chillies, seeded and
  finely chopped
$^1/_2$ cup sliced spring onions

Cut pork into paper-thin bite-sized strips (this is easier if pork is frozen just long enough to make it firm). Unless using instant noodles (follow packet instructions), soak bundles of egg noodles in a bowl of warm water while bringing a pan of lightly salted water to boil. Drain noodles, drop into boiling water and cook for 2 minutes or until just tender. Drain in a colander, run cold water through and drain again. Drizzle 1 tablespoon peanut oil over and mix. Combine sherry and soy sauce.

Heat remaining oil in wok and stir-fry capsicum for 1 minute until colour intensifies. Remove to plate. Add garlic and ginger, and stir-fry until pale golden. Add pork and stir-fry until colour changes. Stir in bean sauce and cook over medium heat for 2 minutes. Add sherry mixture, capsicum and noodles and toss until heated through. Garnish with chillies and spring onions and serve hot.

thai
pork mince with fruit

A meat and fruit salad that makes a really tasty entrée or side dish.

STIR-FRY, **serves 4**

2 tablespoons peanut oil
1 tablespoon Pepper and
    Coriander Paste (see below)
250 g (8 oz) minced pork
2 tablespoons fish sauce
1 tablespoon palm sugar

1 fresh red chilli, chopped
2 oranges
    half a small under-ripe pineapple
$^1/_2$ cup crushed roasted peanuts
$^1/_2$ cup crisp-fried shallots
    fresh mint leaves

Heat oil in wok and fry Pepper and Coriander Paste over low heat, stirring, until it smells fragrant. Add pork and stir-fry until all pork is browned. Add fish sauce, palm sugar, chilli and $^1/_2$ cup water and stir well. Cook quickly until liquid is absorbed, stirring frequently. Turn off heat.

Peel oranges and cut in halves lengthways, then in crosswise slices. Cut away skin and 'eyes' from pineapple and cut lengthways in quarters. Discard core and cut into thin slices. Arrange fruit in a bowl, spooning pork mixture over. Sprinkle with roasted peanuts and fried shallots and garnish with mint leaves. Serve at room temperature.

pepper and coriander paste

A most useful mixture to have on hand when you wish to give your food a Thai flavour.

Keeps for months in a glass jar in the refrigerator. Makes about 1 cup.

1 tablespoon finely chopped garlic
2 teaspoons salt
1 tablespoon whole black
    peppercorns
1 cup firmly packed fresh
    coriander including roots
    and stems
3 tablespoons lime or lemon juice

With the flat of a knife, crush garlic with salt to a smooth paste. Roast peppercorns in a dry wok, stirring, for 2 minutes. Chop coriander finely and put everything into electric blender to purée, adding enough juice to facilitate blending. The paste may also be pounded in a mortar and pestle.

stir-fried beef with mustard cabbage

STIR-FRY, **serves 4**

375 g (12 oz) lean steak
1 tablespoon dry sherry
1 clove garlic, crushed
$^1/_2$ teaspoon oriental sesame oil
1 teaspoon finely grated
** fresh ginger**
2 tablespoons soy sauce
1 teaspoon sugar

1 teaspoon chilli bean sauce
2 tablespoons peanut oil
1 mustard cabbage, stalks cut
** across in thin slices**
1 medium onion, cut lengthwise
** into eighths and layers**
** separated**
1 teaspoon cornflour

Slice steak thinly against grain and cut into bite-sized pieces. Mix meat with sherry, garlic and sesame oil. In a separate small bowl combine ginger, soy sauce, sugar, chilli bean sauce and $^1/_4$ cup water, stirring until sugar is dissolved.

Heat 1 tablespoon oil and stir-fry vegetables over high heat for 2 minutes. Transfer to a dish. Heat remaining oil, add beef and fry over high heat until colour changes. Push beef to side of wok. Add liquid and bring to boil. Add cornflour mixed with 1 tablespoon cold water, stirring until thickened. Stir beef and vegetables through sauce. Serve with steamed rice.

stir-fried beef with vegetables

STIR-FRY, **serves 4**

375 g (12 oz) tender lean beef
1 clove garlic, peeled
salt to taste
1 teaspoon finely grated
fresh ginger
$1/2$ teaspoon five spice powder
2 tablespoons soy sauce

1 green capsicum
1 red capsicum
250 g (8 oz) cauliflower florets
2 tablespoons peanut oil
2 teaspoons cornflour
1 teaspoon oriental sesame oil

Freeze beef until just firm and cut into paper-thin slices. Crush garlic with salt and add to beef with ginger, five spice powder and 2 teaspoons of soy sauce; mix well.

Discard seeds and membranes from capsicums and cut into wide strips, then into diamond shapes. Blanch cauliflower in boiling water for 1 minute. Drain.

Heat wok, add oil and when very hot, add beef and stir-fry until it changes colour. Add capsicums and toss for 1 minute. Add $1/2$ cup water and remaining soy sauce. When liquid comes to boil, push meat and capsicums aside. Mix cornflour with 1 tablespoon of cold water and add to liquid in wok, stirring. It will boil and thicken almost immediately. Add cauliflower, toss meat and vegetables through sauce. Sprinkle with sesame oil and serve immediately with rice.

beef with broccoli

If you like Thai food, here is a dish that will please your tastebuds. Made with either of two pastes, it goes well with steamed rice.

BRAISE, **serves 4**

375 g (12 oz) lean, tender steak
250 g (8 oz) broccoli
2 tablespoons peanut oil
1 tablespoon Pepper and
  Coriander Paste (see p. 64) or
  Red Curry Paste (see p. 54)
1 tablespoon fish sauce

1/2 cup canned coconut milk
2 kaffir lime leaves, fresh, frozen
  or dried
2 teaspoons palm sugar or
  brown sugar
2 red chillies finely sliced
  few fresh basil leaves

Partially freeze beef until firm and cut into thin, bite-sized slices. Divide broccoli into sprigs and blanch in boiling water for 1 minute, drain and refresh in iced water. Drain again.

Heat oil in wok and fry Pepper and Coriander or Red Curry Paste over low heat, stirring, until fragrant. Add beef and stir-fry until coated with paste. Add fish sauce and coconut milk mixed with 1/2 cup water. Stir in kaffir lime leaves and palm sugar and simmer for about 8 minutes. Add broccoli and simmer for 2 minutes or until just tender. Serve sprinkled with finely sliced chilli and fresh basil leaves.

lamb with chilli

Lamb is not usually associated with far-eastern cooking, but if the distinctive flavour is disguised somewhat by lots of chilli and garlic, it is quite acceptable to Asian tastebuds.

STIR-FRY, **serves 4**

500 g (1 lb) lamb fillets
1 teaspoon finely grated
  fresh ginger
4 cloves garlic, crushed
1¹/₂ tablespoons light soy sauce
1 tablespoon medium hot
  chilli sauce

1 tablespoon sherry
1 tablespoon oyster sauce
2 teaspoons sugar
3 tablespoons peanut oil
  half an iceberg lettuce
1 teaspoon oriental sesame oil

Cut lamb into thin slices and rub with ginger, garlic and 2 teaspoons of soy sauce. Combine chilli sauce, sherry, oyster sauce and sugar with 2 tablespoons water and remaining soy, stirring until sugar dissolves.

Heat wok, add 2 tablespoons peanut oil and when hot stir-fry lamb on high heat until it changes colour. Pour in combined sauce mixture, tossing until lamb is browned and coated. Transfer to plate. Wash and dry wok. Cut lettuce in halves lengthways, then cut each half twice vertically and twice horizontally. Add remaining peanut oil to wok and toss lettuce until colour intensifies. Sprinkle with sesame oil, transfer to a serving plate and arrange lamb on top. Serve at once.

indonesian
tasty mince

serves 4

2 tablespoons peanut oil
1 onion, finely chopped
3 cloves garlic, peeled
1 teaspoon salt
1 teaspoon finely chopped
  fresh ginger
2 small red chillies, sliced
3 teaspoons ground coriander

2 teaspoons ground cummin
500 g (1 lb) lean minced steak
$1/4$ teaspoon freshly ground
  black pepper
$1/4$ cup chopped fresh mint
$1/2$ cup finely chopped
  spring onions

Heat oil and fry onion, garlic crushed with salt, ginger and chillies over low heat, stirring until soft. Add coriander and cummin, fry a few seconds longer, then brown steak, breaking it up with cooking spoon and turning it over and over so all meat is browned. Sprinkle with pepper. Cover and simmer until all liquid from meat is absorbed and meat is tender, about 10 minutes. Stir in mint and spring onions for last couple of minutes of cooking and serve with steamed rice and some vegetable accompaniments.

Okay, you knew there had to be a catch somewhere, and here it is. There is something a wok cannot do. I've been singing the praises of this wonderful utensil in which you can boil, braise, fry, simmer or stew. All true. The thing a wok cannot do is cook rice by the absorption method — that needs a pot with a well-fitting lid to hold the steam in. However, when it comes to fried rice and noodles, what else but a wok, with its widely flaring sides, can prevent bits and pieces ending up all over the cooktop. Go ahead and toss with abandon — the wok is ideal for frying and flavouring and adding diced meats to make a meal from rice and noodles.

To cook steamed rice by the absorption method, use a heavy saucepan with a snugly fitting lid. For 500g (2$\frac{1}{2}$ cups) rice, use 3$\frac{1}{2}$ cups water. If necessary, wash the rice and drain it in a colander. Put rice in a saucepan and add water. Bring quickly to boil, cover pan and turn heat very low. Cook for 15 minutes without lifting the lid. The rice will be perfectly cooked and the liquid absorbed.

For fried rice, turn out immediately on to a tray to cool. Refrigerate overnight and you will have firm, separate grains — the perfect starting point.

spring onion and sausage fried rice

Lap cheong are the Chinese equivalent of salami, but with a unique flavour. They need to be steamed until soft before using.

STIR-FRY, **serves 4**

4 **Chinese dried sausages**
  (lap cheong)
2 **tablespoons peanut oil**
2 **cloves garlic, finely chopped**
4 **cups cold steamed rice**
  (see p. 75)
2 **tablespoons light soy sauce**
6 **spring onions, sliced**

Steam lap cheong over boiling water for 10 minutes or until plump and fat is transparent.

(This is easily done in wok, but rinse and dry wok well before adding oil for frying.) Cut lap cheong into thin diagonal slices.

Heat oil in wok, fry garlic for a few seconds, add sliced sausage and toss for 1 minute.

Add rice and stir-fry until grains are separate and lightly coloured. Sprinkle with soy sauce and spring onions and toss to mix and heat through. Serve immediately.

chilli fried rice

STIR-FRY, **serves 4**

3 tablespoons peanut oil
2 medium onions, finely chopped
2 fresh chillies, 1 red and 1 green,
  seeded and sliced finely
2 cloves garlic, finely chopped
250 g (8 oz) boneless pork or
  chicken, finely diced
250 g (8 oz) raw or cooked prawns,
  shelled and deveined
4 cups cold steamed rice
  (see p. 75)
2 eggs, beaten

1 tablespoon light soy sauce
  pepper to taste
2 tablespoons fish sauce
1 tablespoon hot chilli sauce
1 tablespoon fresh lime or
  lemon juice
1 teaspoon sugar
$1/2$ cup chopped spring onions,
  including green tops
$1/2$ cup chopped fresh
  coriander leaves

Heat wok, add oil and fry onions, chillies and garlic until soft, saving a few chilli slices for garnish. Add pork or chicken and stir-fry until cooked. Stir in prawns (roughly chopped if large) and cook until colour changes. Add rice and stir-fry until heated through.

Push rice mixture to side of wok and pour eggs, mixed with soy sauce and pepper into centre. Stir until eggs are set. With wok chan (frying spoon), cut egg into small pieces. Mix fish and chilli sauces, lime juice and sugar and sprinkle over rice. Toss eggs and rice mixture together over high heat for 1 minute. Remove from heat, and toss spring onions and coriander leaves through rice. Garnish with chilli slices and serve immediately.

spring rain noodles with pork

A romantic name for thin, transparent noodles made from mung bean starch. They have no flavour of their own, so do little to mute this dish's fiery flavour.

STIR-FRY, **serves 4**

6 dried shiitake
(Chinese) mushrooms
100 g (3¹/₂ oz) bean thread
vermicelli
3 tablespoons peanut oil
4 spring onions, finely chopped
2 teaspoons finely chopped
fresh ginger
1 teaspoon crushed garlic

250 g (8 oz) minced pork
1 tablespoon dry sherry
1 tablespoon light soy sauce
1 tablespoon hot chilli bean sauce
1 cup chicken stock
2 red chillies, seeded and sliced
fresh coriander leaves
for garnish

Soak mushrooms in hot water for 30 minutes, then discard stems and dice caps finely. Cover noodles with boiling water and soak for 10 minutes or until soft and transparent. Drain in colander, then cut into manageable lengths.

Place wok over high heat. Pour in oil and when hot add spring onions, ginger, garlic, pork and mushrooms. Fry until pork is browned. Stir in sherry, soy and chilli bean sauces. Cook over medium heat for 1 minute. Add stock and when boiling add noodles and cook on low heat until all liquid has been absorbed. Sprinkle with sliced chilli and coriander leaves and serve immediately.

rice

vermicelli with chicken and potato

Potato is not used as a filler or starch component here but deep-fried in tiny dice for texture and flavour.

STIR-FRY, **serves 4-6**

375 g (12 oz) rice vermicelli
250 g (8 oz) chicken breast fillets
1 large raw potato, peeled and
    finely diced
1/4 cup peanut oil
2 large cloves garlic,
    finely chopped

2 medium onions, finely sliced
2 tablespoons light soy sauce
1/4 teaspoon ground black pepper
2 teaspoons sugar
1 tablespoon chilli sauce
    salt to taste
1/2 cup chopped spring onions

Soak rice vermicelli in hot water for 5 minutes, then drain in colander. Cut chicken into bite-sized pieces. Soak diced potato in cold water, drain and dry on paper towels. Heat wok. Pour oil into wok and when a haze rises from surface add diced potato and deep-fry over high heat for 2 minutes. Reduce heat to medium and continue cooking until golden brown and cooked through. Remove with a slotted spoon and set aside.

Pour off oil, leaving about 2 tablespoons. Add garlic and onions and fry for 2 minutes, stirring constantly, over medium heat. Add chicken, stir-fry until flesh turns white. Mix soy sauce, pepper, sugar and chilli sauce into 1/2 cup water, pour into wok and bring to boil. Add rice vermicelli, stir, cover and simmer for 3 minutes or until liquid is absorbed. Mix in potatoes, add salt to taste, sprinkle with spring onions and serve immediately.

fresh rice noodles, singapore style

Stop at any food stall in Singapore and enjoy cha kway teow — rice noodles spiked with chillies and lots of small, tasty tidbits.

STIR-FRY, serves 4-6

500 g (1 lb) fresh rice noodles
(see Note)
3 tablespoons peanut oil
2 teaspoons finely chopped garlic
2 or 3 fresh chillies,
finely chopped
100 g (3½ oz) chopped rump or
fillet steak

2 rashers bacon or ham, chopped
½ cup chicken, chopped
1 cup cooked or frozen green peas
2 teaspoons chilli bean sauce
2 tablespoons oyster sauce
½ cup chopped spring onions
2 teaspoons oriental sesame oil

Cut rice noodles into thin strips and soak in lukewarm water until they separate easily. Drain well.

Heat wok, add oil and fry garlic and chillies, stirring, over medium heat until soft. Add steak, bacon and chicken and stir-fry until cooked. Add peas, chilli bean and oyster sauces and mix well, then add noodles and toss gently to distribute sauces and flavourings. Sprinkle with spring onions and sesame oil and toss a few times to mix. Serve hot.

Note You will find fresh rice noodles called Sa Ho Fun in Asian grocery stores. Use within a day or two. Do not refrigerate, as this makes them hard and brittle.

spicy noodle soup

A meal in one dish, made from bits and pieces you may find in the refrigerator.

BOIL, **serves 2**

2 tablespoons peanut oil
1 small onion, finely sliced
2 tablespoons Pepper and
 Coriander Paste (see p. 64)
2 teaspoons finely grated
 fresh ginger
2 teaspoons ground coriander
$1/2$ teaspoon ground turmeric
4 cups hot chicken stock

1 cup canned coconut milk
2 kaffir lime leaves, fresh or frozen
125 g (4 oz) rice vermicelli
2 small boiled potatoes, sliced
2 hard-boiled eggs, sliced
1 cup cooked chicken, sliced
2 sprigs fresh coriander,
 roughly chopped
crisp fried onions, optional
 (see Note)

Heat oil and over medium-low heat fry onion, Pepper and Coriander Paste, ginger, ground coriander and turmeric, stirring constantly, for about 5 minutes. Add chicken stock, coconut milk and lime leaves and bring to boil. Simmer about 10 minutes. Meanwhile, soak rice vermicelli in hot water for 10 minutes and drain. Drop into simmering soup and cook for 3 or 4 minutes. Serve in soup bowls topped with potatoes, eggs, chicken, coriander and crisp fried onions.

Note Crisp fried onions are available at Asian shops.

ried noodles

Like most Asian dishes, this is a free-wheeling combination, which you can tailor to your taste and availability of ingredients. You will find fresh Hokkien (thick yellow) noodles at Asian supermarkets or you can use dried egg noodles instead. This dish is a meal in itself.

STIR-FRY, **serves 4**

500 g (1 lb) fresh Hokkien mee or
  375 g (12 oz) dried egg noodles
250 g (8 oz) firm bean curd
250 g (8 oz) small raw prawns
3 tablespoons peanut oil
1 onion, finely chopped
5 cloves garlic, finely chopped
2 teaspoons finely chopped
  fresh ginger

1 or more fresh red chillies,
  seeded and sliced
1 teaspoon dried shrimp paste
5 stalks Chinese celery,
  finely sliced
2 tablespoons light soy sauce
$1/2$ cup chopped garlic chives
  thinly sliced cucumber
  lime wedges

Rinse Hokkien noodles in hot water and drain. If using dried noodles, soak in warm water while bringing lightly salted water to boil in a large pan. Drain noodles, drop into boiling water and return to boil for 2 minutes. Noodles must be tender but still firm to bite. Drain immediately in a colander, rinsing with cold water to stop them cooking in their own heat. Drain again.

Cut bean curd into small dice. Shell and devein prawns. Heat oil in wok and fry onion, garlic, ginger and chilli until onion starts to turn golden. Stir in shrimp paste, crushing with back of spoon as it cooks. Add bean curd, prawns and celery, stir-fry until cooked. Add drained noodles and toss to heat. Add soy sauce to taste. Transfer to serving dish and sprinkle with garlic chives. Arrange cucumber slices and lime wedges around edge of dish. Serve with chilli sauce.

glossary

Most of these ingredients are found in Asian stores, although many of them have made their way to supermarket shelves, health shops and the local greengrocer.

Bean Curd
Made from soy beans and high in protein, it is available fresh in various forms — soft, firm, fried. Soft bean curd has the consistency of junket or baked custard, and in Chinese shops is sold immersed in water, whereas Japanese brands are usually called silken tofu and are found in tetra packs. Firm (pressed) bean curd may be found in both yellow and white blocks. Much easier to cook because it does not break up when stirred. Fried bean curd comes in golden brown cubes with a creamy white, spongy interior. Usually sold in plastic bags. All types may be found in the refrigerator section of Asian stores. Fresh bean curd may be kept refrigerated for up to 3 days, but is best when absolutely fresh.
Bean curd is also sold dried and canned. While these have their uses, they should not be substituted for fresh.

Black Beans
Salted, fermented soy beans which come in cans or packets. Rinse away excess salt and use as recipe suggests.

Chilli Bean Sauce
Sold in jars, it is very hot and should be used with discretion.

Chillies
Fresh chillies should be handled with care as the volatile oils can cause much discomfort. Wear gloves, especially when chopping. It is possible to buy fresh chopped chillies in jars and also sambal ulek, which is a mixture of fresh chillies and salt. Dried chillies should be soaked before using. Small chillies are hotter than large ones.

Coconut Milk
Canned coconut milk is readily available but some brands are very thick and rich, others extremely thin. The former should be diluted with water in equal parts, the latter used straight from the can. Usually the thicker ones are more expensive.

Coriander
Coriander seeds and fresh coriander are totally different in flavour and usage. Dried ground coriander seeds are one of the main ingredients in curries. Fresh coriander herb is essential in Thai and Chinese cooking, among others.

Dried Wood Fungus
Also known as 'cloud ear fungus' or 'wood ears' because of its convoluted shape. Resembles bits of black or grey paper in its dried state, but after soaking for 10 minutes or so it swells and turns into translucent brown cloud shapes. A flavourless ingredient used for its texture.

Fish Sauce
A salty sauce used in South-East Asian food.

Five Spice Powder
Spice mixture much loved in Chinese cooking. A combination of ground star anise, fennel, cinnamon, cloves and Szechwan pepper.

Galangal (Alpinia Galanga)
Also known as laos or lengkuas. An aromatic rhizome similar in size and appearance to ginger. May be bought fresh, frozen, dried, ground, or pickled in brine, which is most convenient and keeps indefinitely in the refrigerator.

Garam Masala
Essential in Indian dishes, this is a spice blend worth making up. Roast separately until fragrant: 2 tablespoons coriander seeds, 1 tablespoon cummin seeds, 2 teaspoons whole black peppercorns, 1 teaspoon cardamom seeds (remove from pods), 2 cinnamon sticks and 10 whole cloves. Grind as finely as possible and mix in half a nutmeg, finely grated. Store airtight.

Ginger
Whenever ginger is mentioned in this book, it is fresh ginger root. Now sold at most greengrocers. Dried ground ginger is no substitute.

Hoi Sin Sauce
A thick, dark, sweet and spicy bean sauce used in Chinese dishes. Sold in jars, it keeps indefinitely without refrigeration.

Kaffir Lime Leaves
These are essential in Thai cooking and have a perfume unlike any other citrus leaves. They are sold fresh, frozen and dried.

Ketjap Manis
See Soy sauce.

Lemon Grass
An aromatic plant that grows easily in Australia. The part to use is the white or pale green portion of the stem, which is tender enough to slice finely. Substitute 2 strips thinly peeled lemon rind for each stem of lemon grass.

Maggi Seasoning
A Swiss sauce similar in flavour to Thai Golden Mountain sauce but without added monosodium glutamate, and readily available in western supermarkets.

Mushrooms
Dried Chinese or Japanese mushrooms are the shiitake variety. Their unique flavour cannot be duplicated by dried European mushrooms.

Oyster Sauce
A thick, dark, oyster-flavoured sauce used in Chinese food.

Palm Sugar
Obtained from various tropical palms, this has a distinct flavour. May be substituted by brown sugar.

Sambal Ulek
See Chillies.

Sesame Oil
Whenever sesame oil is called for, use oriental sesame oil made from roasted sesame that is dark in colour and very aromatic. Light coloured sesame oil (usually sold in health food stores) will not impart the same flavour.

Shrimp Paste
Made from dried shrimp, this is powerful stuff. Used in tiny quantities it makes a great difference in flavour and is a mainstay of South-East Asian cuisines. Sold in jars or blocks. Keeps indefinitely.

Soy Sauce
There are many types. For this book you need dark soy (thick, coloured with caramel); light soy (thin, saltier than dark); Indonesian sweetened soy (ketjap manis); and Japanese soy (shoyu). For best results, use the specified kind.

Tamarind
Fruit of a tropical tree, tamarind gives acidity to many dishes. It is sold dried, puréed or instant. The dried pulp has the truest flavour. Soak in hot water, dissolve pulp, strain. Some tamarind is very acidic, so go easy.

Turmeric
The rhizome is dried and ground to a yellow powder that has a distinctive flavour of its own and is used to flavour and colour rice and curries. A staple in commercial curry powders.

index